Curriculum Visions

What do we know about
Jesus?
3: The
Crucifixion

Dr Brian Knapp

In the Garden of Gethsemane.

Notes

There are many translations and adaptations of the Bible. In this book we have sometimes used the King James version, but we have used many other versions and sometimes adapted them, too, depending on which seemed most appropriate for our reading level purpose and for the reading audience.

We have used capital letters to start words that refer to holy people, particularly Jesus or God (Him, He, etc). We have also used capitals when a particular event is implied, such as the Crucifixion of Jesus, but small letters when the general term is implied (e.g. crucifixion). This rule has also been applied to other holy people, such as Disciples (the 12) and disciples (general followers).

The opportunity has been taken to include works of art so that you can see the depiction of events in the eyes of some of the world's most famous historical and modern artists.

Curriculum Visions

There's much more online including videos

You will find multimedia resources covering a wide range of topics at:

www.CurriculumVisions.com

CurriculumVisions is a subscription web site.

A CVP Book © Earthscape 2009

Author
Brian Knapp, BSc, PhD

Researcher
Lisa Magloff, MA

Religious Advisor
The Revd Colin Bass, BSc, MA

Senior Designer
Adele Humphries, BA, PGCE

Editor
Gillian Gatehouse

Designed and produced by
EARTHSCAPE

Printed in China by
WKT Company Ltd

**What do we know about Jesus?
3: The Crucifixion – Curriculum Visions**
A CIP record for this book is available from the British Library

Paperback ISBN 978 1 86214 565 8

Picture credits
All photographs are from the Earthscape and ShutterStock picture libraries or from public domain sources.

This product is manufactured from sustainable managed forests. For every tree cut down at least one more is planted.

⚠ Understanding others

Remember that other people's beliefs are important to them. You must always be considerate and understanding when studying about faith.

Contents

The Passion 4

Jesus enters Jerusalem 6

Jesus at the Temple 8

The Last Supper 11

Jesus is arrested........................... 14

Jesus is tried and convicted....... 16

The Way of the Cross 21

The Resurrection........................... 46

Glossary and Index 48

As you go through the book, look for words in **BOLD CAPITALS**. These words are defined in the glossary.

Veronica wipes Jesus' face with her veil.

Mary weeps by the side of the dead Jesus.

Weblink: www.CurriculumVisions.com

The Passion

The Passion (which means 'suffering') is the Christian word used for the events and suffering of Jesus in the hours just before and including His trial and execution by crucifixion.

The following pages of this book give details about the events leading up to the **CRUCIFIXION**, but it will be easier to see what is going on if you read this summary first. Come back to this page if you get lost at any time. There are several **GOSPEL** versions of the Passion, and this one combines most events that are agreed on.

Most Christians will read the story of the Passion during **HOLY WEEK**, most commonly on Good Friday. It is central to everything Christians believe in.

The Passion has been made into paintings, sculptures, films and many kinds of music, including some of the most famous works of music ever written.

Passion scenes

The Passion story is easiest to understand if it is separated into parts, rather like scenes in a play. There are eight scenes in the Passion, which are summarised here.

1 During a meal a few days before **PASSOVER**, a woman washes and then pours oil over the feet of Jesus. He says she will always be remembered for this.

2 During Passover (on the day we now call Maundy Thursday), Jesus shares the Last Supper with the **DISCIPLES** in a house on the Mount of Olives. Jesus gives final instructions about what the Disciples are to do. He predicts His

betrayal, and tells them all to remember Him. Jesus tells Judas Iscariot to go and do what he must do.

3 After the meal, Jesus and the remaining Disciples walk through the olive groves and enter the Garden of Gethsemane (sometimes known as the Garden of Tears). Jesus tells them they will soon pretend they don't know Him in order to save themselves. After Peter protests that he will not, Jesus says Peter will deny Him three times before the cock crows to usher in the new day.

4 Jesus leaves the Disciples and walks through the garden to pray. The Disciples fall asleep. Then the **TEMPLE** guards arrive with Judas Iscariot, who kisses Jesus on the cheek in order to identify Him. Peter takes a sword and

cuts off the ear of one of the guards, but this does not stop the arrest. The guards give Judas 30 silver coins in payment. They arrest Jesus, and all the others run away, just as Jesus had said.

5 Jesus is taken to the High Priest's palace, and faces charges by the members of the Jewish supreme court (the Sanhedrin). Jesus answers their questions in a way that allow them to say He has **BLASPHEMED**. This is punishable by death, but they cannot authorise that, so they send Him to the court of Pontius Pilate.

6 Meanwhile, in the courtyard outside the High Priest's palace, Peter joins the crowd that has gathered awaiting Jesus' fate; they recognise Peter as a Disciple and begin to get angry, so Peter denies he knows Jesus three times under questioning. As the cock crows, Peter remembers what Jesus had said.

7 Next morning (Good Friday) Pilate, the Roman governor, has Jesus brought before him. Pilate asks Jesus if He is King of the Jews and Jesus replies

'So you say'. Pilate decides that, although Jesus might be a thorn in everyone's side, this does not warrant being put to death. He sends Him to King Herod, who eventually loses patience and sends Him back to Pilate.

The crowd gets angry and Pilate does not want any more trouble. Because it is Passover, Pilate can get out of this by allowing the crowd to choose who to put to death. He offers up a choice between convicted criminal Barabbas or Jesus. Unexpectedly, the crowd choose Jesus to be executed. Pilate sends for water and symbolically washes his hands of the decision as a sign that Jesus' blood would not be upon him. Pilate then sends Jesus out to be crucified. During these events, Jesus is flogged, dressed in a purple robe, in mockery of being a king, and a crown of thorns is placed on His head. Meanwhile, Judas goes and hangs himself.

8 Jesus is forced to carry His cross to the place of execution, a quarry by the hill called Golgotha (also called Calvary) just outside the city walls. Later in the morning Jesus is crucified along with two criminals.

The sky becomes dark at midday and the darkness lasts for three hours, until the ninth hour of the Crucifixion when Jesus cries out "My God, why have You forsaken Me?" Jesus then dies and a soldier pierces His side with a spear just to make sure.

Jesus is then taken down from the cross and buried in a tomb.

Jesus enters Jerusalem

Jesus enters Jerusalem on Palm Sunday in a way that fulfils the prophecies.

On the Sunday before the Passover holiday in springtime, a member of each Jewish family had to go to Jerusalem and make a sacrifice to God at the Temple. Jesus and his Disciples decided to go to Jerusalem even though they all knew danger awaited Jesus there. Up to this point they had been avoiding the place because they knew the **PHARISEES** were laying plans against Jesus.

As they drew close to Jerusalem, Jesus sent two of his Disciples into a nearby village. He told them they would find a donkey, and they should bring it to Him. It was a common custom in many lands in the ancient Middle East to cover the path of someone thought worthy of the highest honour. It was a sort of 'red-carpet' treatment.

Jesus then got on the donkey and rode it into Jerusalem through the Golden Gate. Normally pilgrims would have dismounted. As He rode, Jesus' followers cut (possibly palm) branches from the trees and spread them on the road in His path. The crowd of followers began to shout, "Hosanna to the son of David: Blessed is He that cometh in the name of the Lord; Hosanna in the highest." (Hosanna means 'Save, now')

That Jesus should enter Jerusalem riding on a donkey has many meanings.

Many Christians think it was a sign of humility. The donkey may have been a symbol of peace, as opposed to the horse, which is seen as the animal of war. Therefore, Jesus' entry on a donkey may have been a symbol of peace. However, the Jews saw it quite differently. In the Jewish

▼ Pilgrims recreating part of the walk into Jerusalem on Palm Sunday, carrying palm fronds with them. They are not entering through the Golden Gate as Jesus would have done, because that gate has been sealed for 1,400 years.

▲ A painting showing Jesus arriving on a donkey.

Bible (the Old Testament), the prophet Zachariah prophesies that the **MESSIAH** will enter Jerusalem riding on a donkey:

"Rejoice greatly, O daughter of Zion; shout, O daughter of Jerusalem: behold, thy King cometh unto thee: He is just, and having salvation; lowly, and riding upon a [donkey]..."

To the ruling people this was more like the Messiah's declaration of war against Israel's enemies than a message of peace, because Jewish prophecies say the Messiah will destroy Israel's enemies.

Jesus at the Temple

Jesus preaches in Jerusalem, inflaming even further the anger of the Temple priests. They then plot against Him.

Jesus went to the Temple. Inside the Temple courtyard it was a hive of activity as normal, as people changed money, bought animals for sacrifice and conducted other business. You have to remember that, in past times, people did not behave quietly in a temple or church, that is quite a recent idea. So it wasn't the business itself that Jesus was probably objecting to, but the very high rates that people were charging the poor who came to worship, that is, the businessmen were robbing the poor by not giving them fair value for their money.

▲ Jesus loses His temper with the money-changers in the Temple.

Whatever the reason, we do know that Jesus created a whip from some cords, drove out the livestock, scattered the coins of the money-changers, and turned over their tables, and those of the people selling sacrificial doves. "My house shall be called a house of prayer, but you have made it a den of robbers!" Notice the use of My, means Jesus is saying He is God.

Many people then came up to Jesus in the Temple and asked to be healed, and He healed them.

The next day, Monday, Jesus went back to the Temple and continued His teaching. The crowds around Him grew bigger and the priests became very worried that He was going to cause a rebellion.

Trying to trap Him, the priests asked Jesus, "Teacher, we know that You are honest, and teach the way of God in truth, no matter who You teach, for You aren't biased towards anyone. Tell us therefore, what do You think? Is it lawful to pay taxes to Caesar, or not?"

They were hoping He would say something against taxes that would cause the Romans to arrest Him and save them the trouble.

But Jesus saw through the ruse and said, "Why do you test Me, you hypocrites? Show Me the tax money." They brought Him a Roman coin.

He asked them, "Whose image is on the coin?"

They replied, "Caesar's." (Caesar was the Roman emperor.)

Jesus said, "So give to Caesar that which is Caesar's, and to God the things that are God's," meaning that yes, they should pay their taxes as well as worship God.

The priests then asked Jesus which was the greatest **COMMANDMENT**. Jesus replied, "You shall love the Lord your God with all your heart, with all your soul, and with all your mind." This is the first and greatest commandment. The second is this, "You shall love your neighbour as yourself."

Jesus is anointed with perfume

Following this sermon, Jesus left the Temple and went to the Mount of Olives, where He spoke with His Disciples about His Resurrection and the coming of the Kingdom of God. After this, He went to a nearby village, called Bethany, to spend the night.

While there, a woman came into the house and took a large amount of scented ointment (which was very expensive) and began to rub it on Jesus (some Gospels say she poured it over His head, others that she rubbed it into His feet). Whatever the case, it is the act that is important: it is a sign that the death of Jesus is at hand because such oils were only used to rub over a dead body before burial.

When other people in the room saw this, they said that it was a waste of money. Jesus answered by telling them to leave the woman alone and that she will always be remembered for this act.

He then reminds them that they will always have poor people like this woman with them, but that they will not always have Him. Again, Jesus is telling His Disciples that He will be dead soon.

▼ Christ and the money-changers by Giovanni Paolo Pannini (18th century).

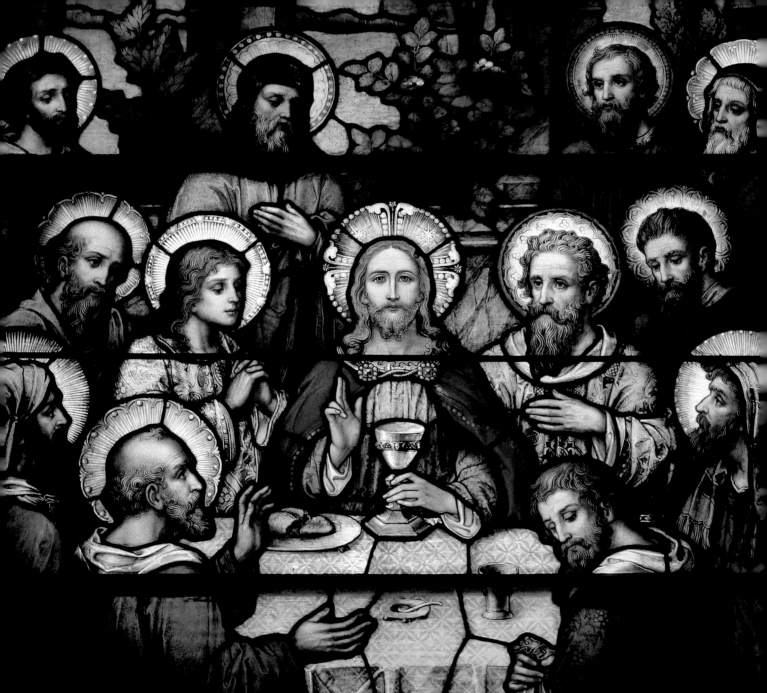

▲ The Last Supper in
a stained glass window.

The Last Supper

This is the time related to the modern Christian communion.

The priests decided it was time to act. While Jesus was in Bethany, one of His Disciples, Judas Iscariot, met with the priests and agreed to hand over Jesus to them. No real reasons are given in the Gospels as to why Judas should hand Jesus over. John implies that he does it for the reward – 30 silver coins, but the other Gospel writers do not say why. However, since Jesus believes He must die in order to save humankind, we can also see Judas' action as necessary and important, not as a simple betrayal at all.

The plot

The priests do not want to arrest Jesus in public, because they are worried about causing unrest, so they agree with Judas that they will wait until Jesus is away from most of the crowds.

The date chosen was the day of the Passover supper (which Jews know as a seder), but it was also when many of the traditions we associate with Christian **COMMUNION** were born. Jesus was starting a new holy day with this meal.

The Jewish holiday of Passover is one of the most important in the Jewish calendar. It commemorates the time when God saved the Jews and brought them out of slavery in Egypt, watched over them in the desert during their long period of wandering, and then brought them to the Promised Land (Israel) and helped them to conquer it.

Communion supper

The holiday lasts for seven days, but on the first two days, people tell the story of Passover, say particular prayers and eat a special meal together. The meal must contain a loaf of unleavened bread called matzah. This meal is eaten in the home, rather than in a synagogue.

What we must remember is that Jesus, as a Jew, had come to Jerusalem to celebrate Passover. So, on the first night of Passover, He gathered with His Disciples to celebrate. But instead of the usual kind of Passover, Jesus took matzah bread, gave thanks for it, and broke it. Then He gave some to each of the Disciples, and told them "This is My body". He then took a cup of wine, gave thanks, and gave it to His Disciples to drink from, telling them "This is My blood".

Here, Jesus is starting a new ceremony. He is telling His Disciples that if they share bread and wine in the spirit of Christ, that the spirit of Christ will enter them and their sins will be forgiven. This is the origin of the communion ceremony in Christianity.

After the meal was eaten, Jesus took off His cloak and washed His Disciples' feet. When they protested, He told them that if they did not let Him wash their feet, they could not be His followers, so they allowed Jesus to wash their feet, and then they washed each other's feet. This was an act of humbleness and it was a reminder that all should be humble in the eyes of God.

Jesus then told His Disciples that one of them would hand Him over to the Temple guards. They all protested, but Jesus said that He would break a piece of bread and dip it in salt water and whoever He handed it to is the person. He did this and handed the bread to Judas, saying, "Go, quickly." Judas left and went out to meet the Temple guards.

The New Commandment

After Judas left, Jesus told his Disciples that He would be leaving them soon, but He was giving them a New Commandment,

Pictures of the Last Supper

Very many fine pictures have been made of the Last Supper and some are on these pages. However, these were mainly painted in times when people were not interested in historical accuracy. To be accurate, the supper would have been taken around a three-sided low table, with Jesus at one end. The people would all have reclined on couches and leaned on one elbow, using the other arm to serve themselves the food they needed. It was not at all as you see in these paintings but that, of course, does not affect the message.

that of loving one another. The Disciple Simon Peter then asked Jesus where He was going. Jesus answered that where He was going they could not follow for the moment, but that they would follow later (meaning after they died).

It was at this point that Peter asked why he could not follow his Lord immediately for he would lay down his life for Him. Jesus then tells Peter that although he has said this, Peter will presently deny knowing Jesus three times before the cock crows at the next dawn.

The Holy Spirit

Jesus told his Disciples that He and God are one, and that the way to know God and be saved is to follow Jesus' teachings; that those who follow Jesus' teachings and believe in Him will be granted what they wish. To know Jesus is to know God. The way to think about this, Jesus tells them, is to liken Himself and people to a vine:

I am the true vine, and My Father is the husbandman. Every branch in Me that beareth not fruit He taketh away: and every branch that beareth fruit, He purgeth it, that it may bring forth more fruit. Now ye are clean through the word which I have spoken unto you.

Abide in Me, and I in you. As the branch cannot bear fruit of itself, except it abide in the vine; no more can ye, except ye abide in Me. I am the vine, ye are the branches: He that abideth in Me, and I in him, the same bringeth forth much fruit: for without Me ye can do nothing.

Jesus then tells them that the greatest love is the willingness to lay down one's life for one's friends. This passage has been widely used to explain the sacrifice of martyrs and soldiers in war, and is often seen on war memorials and graves.

Jesus then says that He will send a comforter, a Spirit of Truth, a Holy Spirit, which would help them in their task of continuing to spread Jesus' teachings. Jesus then warned His Disciples that they would meet with hatred and resistance, as He had.

Jesus warned them that He would be leaving them now, but they should not worry, because if He didn't leave, the Spirit would not come to them and so they would not be able to spread His teachings. In other words, it is only through His death that His teachings can be spread.

Jesus then prayed for Himself, for the Disciples and for all believers.

Then Jesus and the Disciples left the house where they were having the Passover meal and went to the Garden of Gethsemane, where they had often prayed together before.

▲ **The Last Supper by Leonardo da Vinci.**

Jesus is arrested

Jesus is arrested in the Garden of Gethsemane.

Once in the Garden of Gethsemane, also called the Garden of Tears by some, Jesus told His Disciples to keep watch while He went a little way off and prayed.

It had been a long night and they had eaten and drank well, so the Disciples fell asleep. He came back and awoke them twice. On the third time, when Jesus found them sleeping, He said, "Sleep on now, and take your rest: behold, the hour is at hand, and the Son of Man is betrayed into the hands of sinners. Rise, let us be going: behold, he is at hand that doth betray Me."

While Jesus was speaking this, Judas and the Temple guards arrived. Judas had earlier told the guards that he would give Jesus a kiss, so the guards would know who He was. Now Judas walked up to Jesus and gave Him a kiss.

Jesus said to him, "Friend, do what you are here to do."

When his Disciples saw the soldiers arrest Jesus, Peter drew a sword and struck one of the guards, cutting off his ear.

But Jesus told the Disciples to put away their swords, and told them that all those who live by the sword will die by the sword. Jesus reminded

▼ Judas' kiss, Giotto.

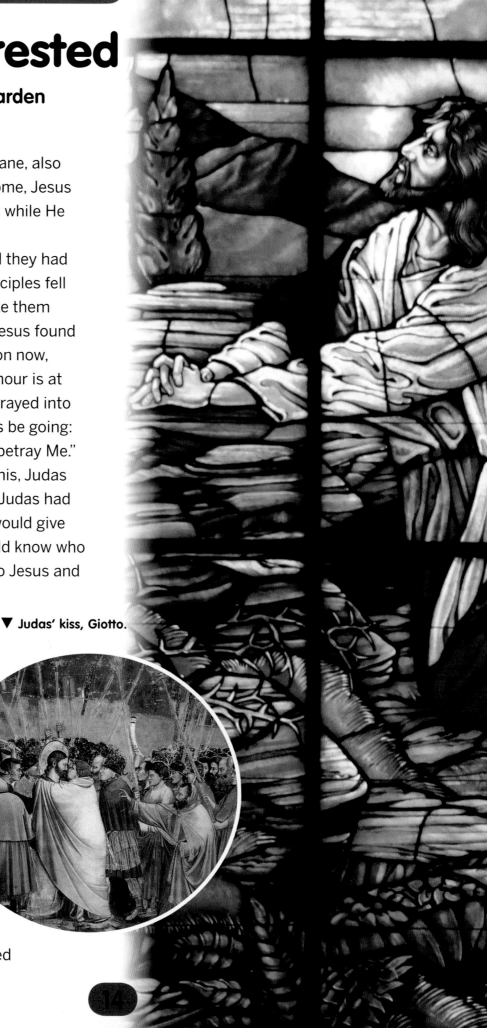

▲ While in the Garden of Gethsemane, Jesus is believed to have sweated drops of blood.

◀ A stained glass window showing Jesus praying to His Father in the Garden of Gethsemane while the Disciples sleep.

his Disciples that it was time for Him to die, to fulfil the scriptures, and nothing would save Him now.

Jesus then asked the guards why they had come in the night as though He was a robber, brandishing swords and clubs. He reminded them that He had sat daily in the Temple teaching when it would have been easy to arrest Him, but they didn't. He was reminding them that they were cowards. Of course, they had no answer to this because they were just doing their job. But by now it was clear that they were going to arrest Jesus and the Disciples stopped trying to protect Him. Instead, they left Him and fled, hoping not to be caught up in the arrest, too.

Jesus is tried and convicted

The priests condemn Jesus while out of public sight.

When it came to arresting and killing Jesus, the priests had a real problem. Remember, in lands conquered by the Romans the people had to pay taxes, provide soldiers for Rome's campaigns and follow Roman law. Although a Roman governor was in charge, the locals still governed themselves in day-to-day life and in local affairs. However, any rebellion against Roman rule was punished severely: by massacre, loss of freedom and sometimes entire populations were sold off into slavery. It was not in the interests of the priests to allow an uprising that might have affected their comfortable positions. So they probably had a political motive, as well as a religious one, for getting rid of Jesus.

Even if the Jewish leaders had political rather than religious motives, they first accused Jesus of **BLASPHEMY** because it was a charge they thought they could make stick. It was to be what we now call a 'show trial'. Jesus was arrested at night and taken immediately to be tried in front of one of the senior priests, Annas.

Annas

Annas asked Jesus about His teachings. Jesus answered him, "I spoke openly to the world. I always taught in synagogues, and in the Temple, where the Jews always meet. I said nothing in secret. Why do you ask Me? Ask those who have heard Me what I said to them. Behold, these people know the things which I said."

Jesus was pointing out that He had always been honest about who He was and what He was teaching.

Annas may have been looking for Jesus to apologise, and save Caiaphas, the High Priest, the trouble of condemning Him, but these words made it clear that Jesus believed He had done nothing wrong. So Annas sent Jesus on to Caiaphas, the High Priest.

▼ The trial of Jesus, St John the Baptist church, Yaroslavl.

Jesus is tried by Caiaphas

Now the priests were busily looking for witnesses who could show that Jesus had committed blasphemy and so should be put to death. But no one would step forward. The priests needed an airtight case, to avoid a riot, and so Caiaphas stood up and asked Jesus, "Have you no answer to the charges? But Jesus said nothing. So he asked Jesus, "Tell me, are You the Christ, the Son of God?"

Jesus said, "I am. You will see the Son of Man sitting at the right hand of God, and coming with the clouds of the sky."

In the eyes of the court Jesus had now committed blasphemy. No more witnesses were needed.

However, Caiaphas had a real problem. The Romans had temporarily removed from the Jewish leaders the right to execute anyone for anything (because they had used it too freely) so the Jewish leaders had to take Jesus before Roman governor Pilate if they wanted Jesus killed. Pilate would hardly have cared about anyone committing blasphemy – just another religious squabble among fanatically religious people. He would not have imposed the death penalty for it, even though the Jewish leaders would have done if they could. So the Jewish leaders changed the charge to 'causing an uprising against the Roman Empire'. If Jesus had claimed to be a king, He was challenging the authority of Rome, and Pilate would take that very seriously if it was proved.

So Caiaphas decided that Jesus should go to governor Pontius Pilate with a recommendation that He be put to death.

▼ Peter denies Jesus three times before the cock crows.

Punishment

Peter had followed the guards as they brought Jesus before Annas and Caiaphas. As Jesus was being interviewed, Peter was standing around in the courtyard with many other people. It was a cold night and they were all warming themselves by a fire. As they were all standing around, a woman said she thought she recognised Peter and asked him if he had been with Jesus. But Peter said no, he was not with Jesus. He was afraid of what the mob would do to him.

Peter moved away a bit, but someone else then said, "This man was with Jesus of Nazareth."

But again Peter denied it, saying, "I don't know the man."

After a little while some more people came and said to Peter, "Surely you are also one of them, for your voice sounds familiar."

Peter, in a panic, yelled out, "I don't know the man!"

Just then a cock crowed and Peter suddenly remembered that Jesus had said to him: "Before the cock crows, you will deny Me three times." Realising what he had done, Peter left the group and wept bitterly.

Judas hangs himself

Judas also had regrets that night for what he had done even though it had been necessary for God's plan.

After Jesus had been condemned by the priests, Judas felt so guilty he went to the chief priests and gave them back their 30 pieces of silver, saying , "I have sinned, I betrayed an innocent man." Then Judas threw the coins at the feet of the priests and went to a field and hung himself.

Pilate

The Roman governor, Pilate, had a tough job because Judea was an unruly region and Pilate's job was to be a politician and keep things under control. So although Pilate was not especially anxious to kill Jesus, he knew that if he upset the priests, they would make trouble for him as well. Let's be clear: Pilate was not squeamish about putting people to death or curbing a rebellion, but it looks bad in Rome when your province rebels, and it's bad for the tax revenues as well.

Pilate was called to deal with this in the early hours of the morning and we can imagine he was not in the best of moods.

Pilate had Jesus brought inside his house and asked Him, "Are you the King of the Jews?"

Jesus answered him, "Do you say this by yourself, or did others tell you about Me?"

Pilate answered, "I'm not a Jew, am I? Your own people and the chief priests delivered You to me."

By asking if Jesus thought He was a king, Pilate wanted to know if Jesus would proclaim Himself king and lead a rebellion against Roman rule. But Jesus dodges the question. Pilate then went back outside and told the priests, "I find no basis for a charge against this man."

But the priests insisted, saying, "He stirs up the people, teaching throughout all Judea, beginning from Galilee to Jerusalem." When Pilate heard Galilee mentioned he asked if Jesus was a Galilean. That put Jesus in King Herod's (Herod the Great's son) jurisdiction. So Pilate sent Jesus on to Herod, who happened to be in Jerusalem for Passover.

When Jesus arrived at Herod's house, Herod asked Him to perform a miracle, but Jesus said nothing. When Jesus refused to speak, Herod and his soldiers teased Jesus, then Herod dressed Him in luxurious clothing – as a sort of mock king – and sent Him back to Pilate.

The final decision

So Jesus is back at Pilate's house, and it is now obvious to Pilate that all of the Jewish leaders want Jesus dead. Yet he is still loathe to put Jesus to death for what he sees as nothing serious.

Pilate called together the chief priests and the rulers and the people, and said to them, that neither he nor Herod had found anything against Jesus and so he proposed

▲ Pilate orders Jesus to be taken away and flogged.

simply to whip and release Him. So Jesus was taken away and flogged. After the flogging, the soldiers placed a crown of thorns on His head, mocking the idea of Jesus as the King of the Jews.

After He was flogged, Jesus was again brought out to Pilate, the chief priests and the leaders, who began shouting at Pilate to sentence Jesus to death. But Pilate was convinced Jesus did not deserve death and he gave the crowd one more chance to save Jesus.

At Passover, it was the custom for the Roman governor to grant clemency to one prisoner. So Pilate now sat down on his judge's seat and asked the crowd who they would like released, the proven criminal Barabbas, or Jesus.

The chief priests and the elders whipped the crowd up against Jesus, so they shouted for Pilate to release Barabbas. Pilate then asked them what he should do with Jesus, and the crowd shouted "Crucify Him!"

At this, Pilate gave up. He could see that the priests had whipped up the crowd and nothing more could be done. Pilate had a bowl of water brought to him and he washed his hands in front of the crowd, saying, "I wash my hands of this matter. It is done."

The solders immediately grabbed Jesus and led Him off for crucifixion. It was Friday afternoon.

▲ Many people try to recreate
the atmosphere of the last
journey of Jesus along the
Sorrowful Way, the Via Dolorosa.

The Way of the Cross

The last stages of the life of Jesus are often summarised in the 14 Stations of the Cross.

Now we come to the end of Jesus' time on Earth. Many Christians commemorate this time by remembering 14 events that traditionally tell about what happened from the time Jesus is condemned to die, until He is laid in the tomb. These events are called the Stations of the Cross.

The word 'station' stems from Latin '*statio*', meaning: I stand (to pray). As far back as the 16th century these stations could be seen along the street called the Via Dolorosa (also known as the Road of Sorrows and The Sorrowful Way) in Jerusalem, a well-known journey for pilgrims ever since.

In the early centuries of Christianity, Christians would walk the streets of Jerusalem, stand at each point, pray and remember what Jesus went through. In fact, one tradition is that the practice of walking the route started because Mary walked the route that Jesus took on His way to death every day, kneeling and praying at several places along the way.

When Jerusalem was conquered by Muslims in the 8th century, it was no longer safe for pilgrims to come to Jerusalem. So at home, they made plaques, statues or other images of the places and events and placed them around churches at home, so people could still pray and remember what happened to Jesus in those last hours. That is one reason why many churches now have pictures of the 14 stations. You will see one set from a church in these pages. Not all of the events we remember today as stations are found in the Bible. Some of them come from people's memories or from tradition.

The 14 traditional stations are:
1. **Jesus is condemned to die**
2. **Jesus is made to bear His cross**
3. **Jesus falls the first time**
4. **Jesus meets His mother**
5. **Simon helps Jesus carry His cross**
6. **Veronica wipes Jesus' face**
7. **Jesus falls the second time**
8. **Jesus meets the women of Jerusalem**
9. **Jesus falls the third time**
10. **Jesus is stripped**
11. **Jesus is nailed to the cross**
12. **Jesus dies on the cross**
13. **Jesus is taken down from the cross**
14. **Jesus is laid in the tomb**

However, because there is no record of many of these events in the Bible and they can be sources of confusion and controversy, Pope John Paul II introduced a new form of devotion, called the Scriptural Way of the Cross on Good Friday 1991. In 2007, Pope Benedict XVI approved this set of stations for meditation and public celebration.

The events in the Scriptural Way of the Cross are:

1. Jesus in the Garden of Gethsemane
2. Jesus is betrayed by Judas and arrested
3. Jesus is condemned by the Jews (Sanhedrin)
4. Jesus is denied by Peter
5. Jesus is judged by Pilate
6. Jesus is scourged and crowned with thorns
7. Jesus takes up His cross
8. Jesus is helped by Simon to carry His cross
9. Jesus meets the women of Jerusalem
10. Jesus is crucified
11. Jesus promises His Kingdom to the good thief
12. Jesus entrusts Mary and John to each other
13. Jesus dies on the cross
14. Jesus is laid in the tomb

These are the stations the Pope uses when he does a public ceremony at Easter in Rome. However, most people follow the traditional stations and use these new stations as an additional form of devotion.

For most pilgrims, the exact location of each event along the Via Dolorosa is of little importance; it is the events they remember that have the meaning.

Today, the Via Dolorosa winds through crowded, narrow streets, paved with stones worn smooth from centuries of use, and lined with store fronts. Today, the stores sell mostly souvenirs, while in Jesus' time they would have sold everyday goods, but in many other respects the Via Dolorosa has changed little down the centuries.

The route of the Via Dolorosa begins near the Lions' Gate in the old walled city, next to the ancient Roman fort and Jewish Temple. (This is now in the Muslim Quarter.) The route ends at the Church of the Holy Sepulchre (now in the Christian Quarter). It is a short way... a mere 500 metres. Each of the 14 traditional Stations of the Cross along the Via Dolorosa is marked with a small plaque.

▼ The Via Dolorosa as it is today.

The Passion

The Passion is the term used for the events and suffering of Jesus in the hours before and during His trial and execution by crucifixion.

The term the Agony of Jesus refers to the Agony in the Garden, when Jesus prayed before His arrest in the Garden of Gethsemane.

Those parts of the four Gospels that describe these events are known as the 'Passion narratives'. The Gospel of Peter also contains a Passion narrative.

▲ The Via Dolorosa on Palm Sunday.

The First Station

Jesus is condemned to die

This is the first stage leading to the Crucifixion and occurred when the Roman governor, Pontius Pilate, publicly condemned Jesus to death. He did this at his official residence in the fort, a building called the praetorium.

In Jesus' day, the Passover holiday was a popular time for riots and uprisings. As a result, Pilate was here with his soldiers in case of trouble.

The praetorium had a large indoor courtyard for private audiences and a large outdoor courtyard for hearing petitions and addressing crowds.

You will remember that Jesus had now been put in front of the Jewish Temple High Priest, Caiaphas, King Herod and Roman governor Pilate. It was during these interviews that Jesus was flogged, tied up and had a crown of thorns placed on His head in mockery of what the priests said

▲ Station 1

about Jesus being King of the Jews (a claim He never made).

Pilate then brought Jesus out to the crowd gathered outside the praetorium who were shouting for Jesus' death and said, "Behold the man". He was showing that he had punished Jesus.

But the crowd were not satisfied. The priests had roused them up into a frenzy and they shouted, "Crucify Him, crucify Him!" This was not something Pilate wanted to do, but he had forced himself into a corner and had to condemn Jesus to death. But at the same time, he wanted to make clear that it was not with his blessing. So Pilate sat down on his official seat of judgement. Then he took a bowl of water, washed his hands, and said, "I wash my hands of this matter. It is done."

It was these words that began Jesus' walk to Golgotha, also called Calvary. He had been arrested only the night before, and He would be dead by sunset.

▲ The edge of Pilate's praetorium marks the beginning of The Sorrowful Way.

◄ People touching one of the Stations of the Cross in Jerusalem.

The Second Station

Jesus is made to bear His cross

This station gives a chance to think about what Jesus might have thought as He waited to begin His final walk.

As soon as the sentence was pronounced, word spread through the crowd. As in later centuries, a public execution was a popular event. In this case there were to be three executions: Jesus and two thieves.

Some people in the crowd were happy – they thought that at last the troublemaker would be taken care of. Others were simply enjoying the show and a crucifixion was a big event. But there were many in the crowd who were deeply saddened and stunned. None of the Disciples were present, and we can imagine that they were terrified they would be next. In a few weeks, the Holy Spirit would descend on them, but at this terrible time they were just confused.

▲ Station 2

Jesus and the two others were prepared for crucifixion in the main courtyard of the praetorium. Although Jesus is usually pictured carrying the entire cross, in reality the Romans only made the condemned man carry the crossbar. The upright piece was already in place at the site of the crucifixion.

The two thieves and Jesus were tied to their crossbars in the courtyard and then the gates of the fortress were opened. The escorting soldiers came out and in the middle of them were the condemned prisoners. But Jesus had already been through an horrific ordeal and so He was weak and He could hardly stand on His own feet.

As Jesus gazed to His left, on the way out of the praetorium, He would have seen the perimeter walls of the Temple, and in front of Him the road leading to the gate outside the city. He would have seen many faces enjoying the show. Only a few of the people lining the road were crying.

Between the Second and Third Stations is an arch spanning the Via Dolorosa. It is called the Ecce Homo Arch (which is Latin for the words Pilate uttered "Behold the man"). The Ecce Homo Basilica (church) is on one side of the arch and the Ecce Homo Convent is nearby.

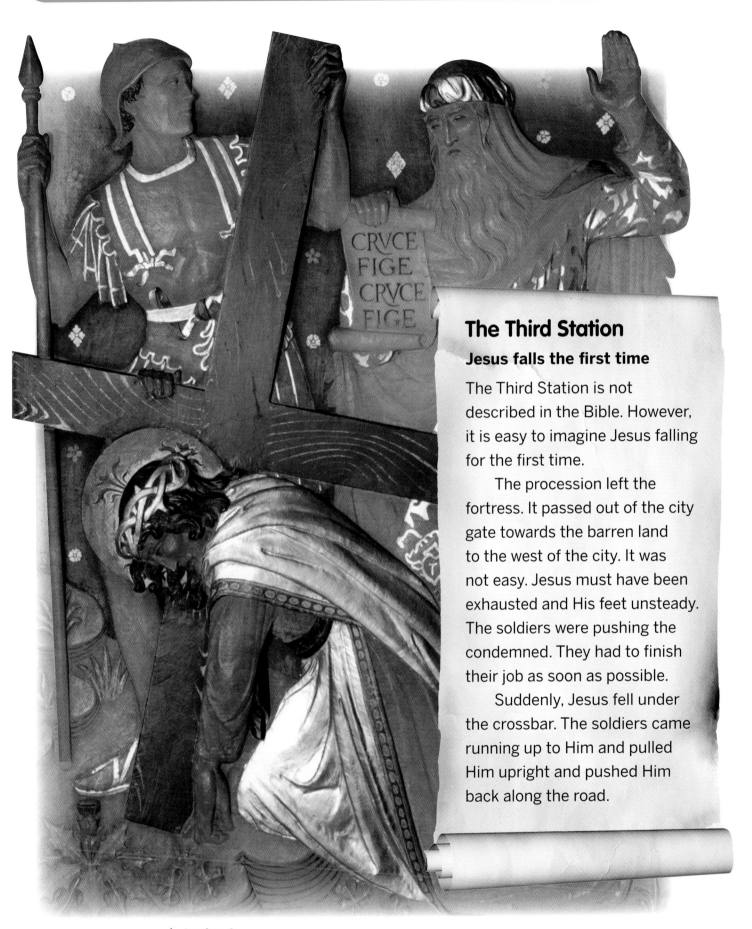

The Third Station
Jesus falls the first time

The Third Station is not described in the Bible. However, it is easy to imagine Jesus falling for the first time.

The procession left the fortress. It passed out of the city gate towards the barren land to the west of the city. It was not easy. Jesus must have been exhausted and His feet unsteady. The soldiers were pushing the condemned. They had to finish their job as soon as possible.

Suddenly, Jesus fell under the crossbar. The soldiers came running up to Him and pulled Him upright and pushed Him back along the road.

▲ Station 3

The Fourth Station

Jesus meets His mother

Although it is not in the Bible, many people believe that Mary, Jesus' mother, had come to see her son one last time, and it was at a spot shortly after He fell that she waited to catch a last glimpse of Him.

We can imagine her standing at the side of the road, along with some other women followers of Jesus and family members. She would have wanted to talk to Jesus, but she could not. Perhaps Jesus paused and was pushed away again by the soldiers.

The Fifth Station

Simon helps Jesus carry His cross

The road begins to go uphill. Although it is not very steep, it was too much for the exhausted Jesus. He had already fallen once and was probably trembling again at this point. It did not look like He was going to make it. But the soldiers did not want Him dying before He was crucified — the whole point of crucifixion was to demonstrate Roman power by making the victim suffer.

The soldiers had to make sure Jesus got to the execution site. So they looked around. Simon of Cyrene and his sons were on their way into Jerusalem from the countryside. A road leading into the city from the country once crossed the main road at the site of the Fifth Station.

This is why Simon was in the crowd when the soldiers grabbed him. Simon looked strong, so they made him carry Jesus' crossbar the rest of the way.

Simon became a follower of Jesus and although he was forced to carry the bar of the cross, we can imagine

▲ Station 5

he would have been glad of the chance to help Jesus in any way he could.

Today, there is a small Franciscan chapel at the site.

Weblink: www.CurriculumVisions.com

▲ A mosaic of the impression left by the face of Jesus on the veil of Veronica (now St. Veronica) at the Sixth Station.

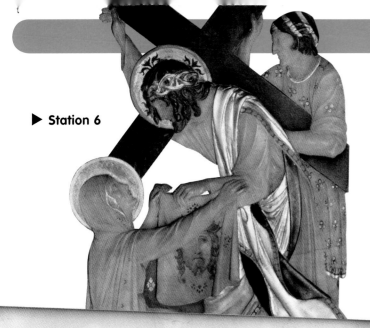

▶ Station 6

The Seventh Station
Jesus falls the second time

The way uphill becomes even more difficult at this point. Jesus is weak. He again falls to the ground and is put back on His feet by the soldiers.

Today, there is a Franciscan chapel on the site of the Seventh Station.

The Sixth Station
Veronica wipes Jesus' face

At the Sixth Station, the procession had started an uphill climb and the top of the hill, Calvary, could already be seen in the west standing out against the sky.

According to tradition, suddenly, a woman ran out of the crowd, tore off her veil and handed it to Jesus so that He could wipe the sweat and blood from His face. This was dangerous, as the soldiers were likely to treat her roughly, but she did not think about her safety. She saw Jesus' suffering and thought that this might help a little. Jesus accepted the offering and after using it handed it back to her, the image of His face miraculously left upon it.

The woman is believed to have been called a name which got handed down as Veronica. Veronica helps to show that anyone can have compassion and that this will be rewarded, even in this life (Veronica was given the gift of the veil that cures illness).

A Greek Catholic Church stands at the Sixth Station.

▲ Station 7

31

The Eighth Station

Jesus meets the women of Jerusalem

The Bible tells us that a large number of people followed Jesus along His walk to death, including a number of women who were weeping and mourning Jesus. When Jesus sees these women, He turns to them and says, "Daughters of Jerusalem, weep not for Me, but weep for yourselves, and for your children."

With these words, Jesus is prophesying the destruction of Jerusalem, which He had warned about many times. He is saying that, in the coming times people will have to watch their children die and so would be better off without children. He is warning that there will come a time when people will desperately hide in the mountains and the hills.

The people are seeing the death of Jesus now, when there is peace, but what will they do when there is war – what horrors will they have to witness then?

In this message, Jesus is once again telling people that it is time to repent and to follow His teachings, before it is too late. In His final moments, Jesus is not thinking of Himself, but of others and is urging them to follow His teachings while they can.

Jesus reaches Calvary

At Calvary, Jesus falls a third time, is stripped and nailed to the cross

The last stations are all inside the Church of the Holy Sepulchre. Sepulchre means tomb. It is the church built over the tomb in which Jesus was laid to rest. The Church of the Holy Sepulchre (the church of the holy tomb) was built on the site of both Jesus' Crucifixion and burial. This seems a bit odd today, as the church is in a busy area in the middle of the Old City. But in Jesus' day, this hill was outside the city walls of the time. This hill was called Golgotha (the place of skulls), or Calvary, and was the traditional site of crucifixions.

As Jesus foretold, the Jewish Temple was destroyed, first in 70 AD and more thoroughly in 135 AD. The Jews were also thrown out of Jerusalem. As a final insult, Emperor Hadrian built a temple to the Roman goddess Venus on the Crucifixion site. However, in later years, the Emperor Constantine (who, like many Romans, was a Christian), took down the temple and put a church (basilica) on the site. Although this church was destroyed in 1006, it was rebuilt in 1027–28 and it is that building that remains today.

▶ The tomb (sepulchre) of Jesus is within the Church of the Holy Sepulchre and inside this box-like structure.

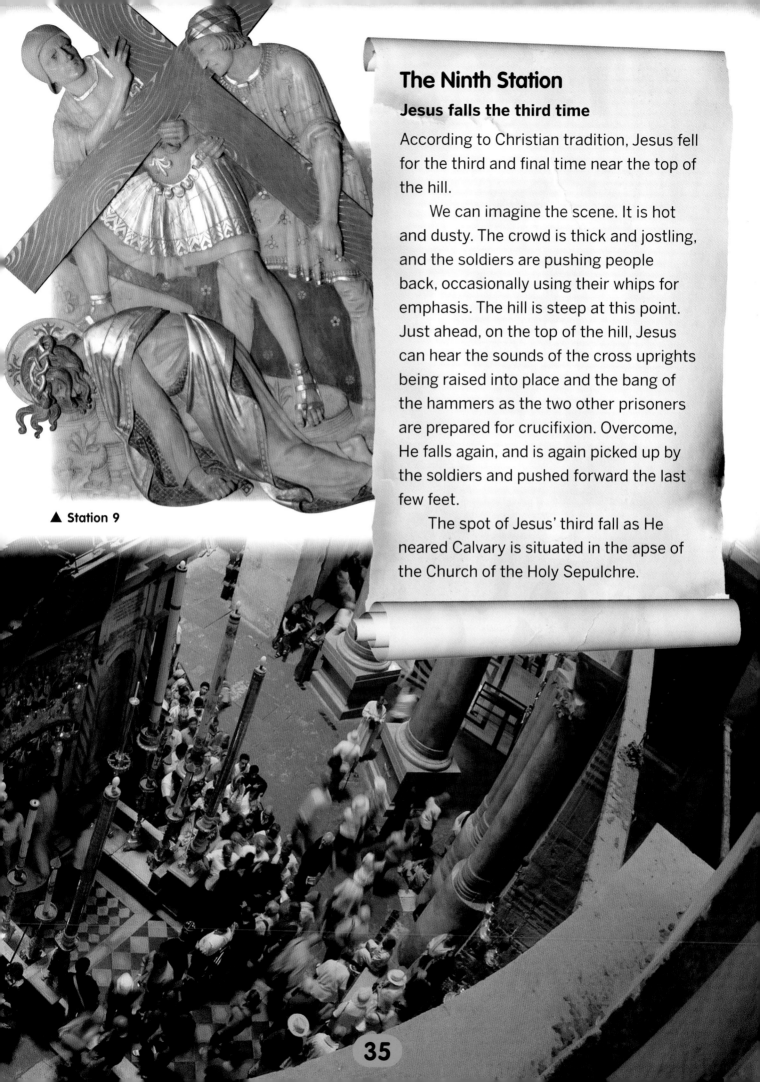

The Ninth Station

Jesus falls the third time

According to Christian tradition, Jesus fell for the third and final time near the top of the hill.

We can imagine the scene. It is hot and dusty. The crowd is thick and jostling, and the soldiers are pushing people back, occasionally using their whips for emphasis. The hill is steep at this point. Just ahead, on the top of the hill, Jesus can hear the sounds of the cross uprights being raised into place and the bang of the hammers as the two other prisoners are prepared for crucifixion. Overcome, He falls again, and is again picked up by the soldiers and pushed forward the last few feet.

The spot of Jesus' third fall as He neared Calvary is situated in the apse of the Church of the Holy Sepulchre.

▲ Station 9

The Tenth Station

Jesus is stripped

Now Jesus arrives at the foot of Calvary (or Golgotha). Perhaps Jesus looks up and sees the two thieves already in their place on the cross. They are screaming with pain.

The soldiers take off Jesus' clothes, leaving Him with just a loin-cloth. We can imagine that the clothes were mostly rags at this point anyway.

People were usually crucified in just a loin-cloth. This was not done to embarrass them, but to speed up their death by exposing them to the elements.

Later the soldiers took Jesus' clothes and divided them into four piles, with each soldier taking one pile. They were mostly rags, but even rags had some value. The purple cloak, which had been put on Jesus in jest, was too nice to tear up, so the soldiers cast lots for it.

When you enter the main door of the church of the Holy Sepulchre, a stairway on your right takes you to the spot where Jesus was stripped and placed on the cross. The Tenth Station is located at the beginning of a nave on the right.

The Tenth Station events have been a popular topic for painters through the ages. Here, the executioners, having violently stripped Jesus of His garments, which had fastened to His wounds, lead Him to the Cross.

It was a custom of the Romans to strip to the loin-cloth those who were to die on the cross.

This is part of one of the most famous paintings of this scene. It was painted by the artist called El Greco in the 16th century. Notice that the soldiers are dressed in the armour used at the time of the painting, that is Spanish conquistador armour and they carry Spanish-style pikes, not the dress at the time of Jesus. The red-purple robe of Jesus represents divine passion. El Greco chooses to make Jesus tall and serene and His captors are made to look brutal.

▼ Station 10

▼ Station 11

Pater dimitte illis

The Eleventh Station

Jesus is nailed to the cross

The punishment of crucifixion was the fixing of the person to a cross. Some victims were tied up, others nailed up. Jesus was nailed up. Crucifixion was a slow death, but this suffering was usually not intended to last for more than a few hours. Certain things were done in order to speed up the process. It was hot and dry in Jerusalem, and exposure to the sun would have helped speed up Jesus' death.

The cross beam was placed on the ground and Jesus was laid on it, forced to lie face up with His arms outstretched. The soldiers nailed His arms to the cross and He was lifted into place on the upright. Then His feet were nailed into place.

The legs would probably have been bent at the knees and turned to one side, and there would have likely been a small ledge on the upright to sit on and partly take the weight so that the nails did not pull through the flesh. With the legs twisted, and the arms out like this, it is difficult to breath and the victim would eventually have suffocated.

According to John, Pilate had a sign written in Hebrew, Latin and Greek which was nailed to the cross and read "Jesus of Nazareth, King of the Jews." The chief priest complained when he saw this. He felt the sign should have read, "He said, I am King of the Jews." But Pilate answered, "What I have written, I have written."

We can easily see why the priest is complaining. The words "He said" indicate that Jesus committed blasphemy and that is why He was being killed. The words "Jesus of Nazareth, King of the Jews" imply that Jesus was in fact the Messiah.

Jesus looked down and saw His mother, and His mother's sister, Mary, Mary Magdalene and the Disciple John standing near the foot of the cross. Jesus said to His mother, "Woman, behold your son!" Then He said to John, "Behold, your mother!"

Jesus was entrusting His mother into John's care. Jesus intended that from now on, Mary should look on John as her son and John would look on Mary as his own mother.

The Twelfth Station

Jesus dies on the cross

The crowd were still jeering and mocking Jesus. People laughed at Him, saying, "You claim You can heal others, why can't You heal Yourself. If You are the King of the Jews, then come down from the cross and we'll believe You."

Suddenly, after many hours, the soldiers heard Jesus cry out, "My God, My God, why have You forsaken Me?" Jesus also cried out "I thirst". The soldiers took a sponge and soaked it in vinegar and a herb, put the sponge on the end of a spear or stick and offered it to Jesus to drink. The soldiers, seeing the end was near, were probably offering Jesus some sour wine mixed with a drug. This was common practice, again, to speed the end as both the Sabbath and the start of the Passover festival were approaching. With the senses dulled, the victim would stop fighting and give up.

Jesus then cried out, "It is finished," and died.

▼ Jesus is taken down from the Cross.

▼ Jesus is taken down from the Cross.

42

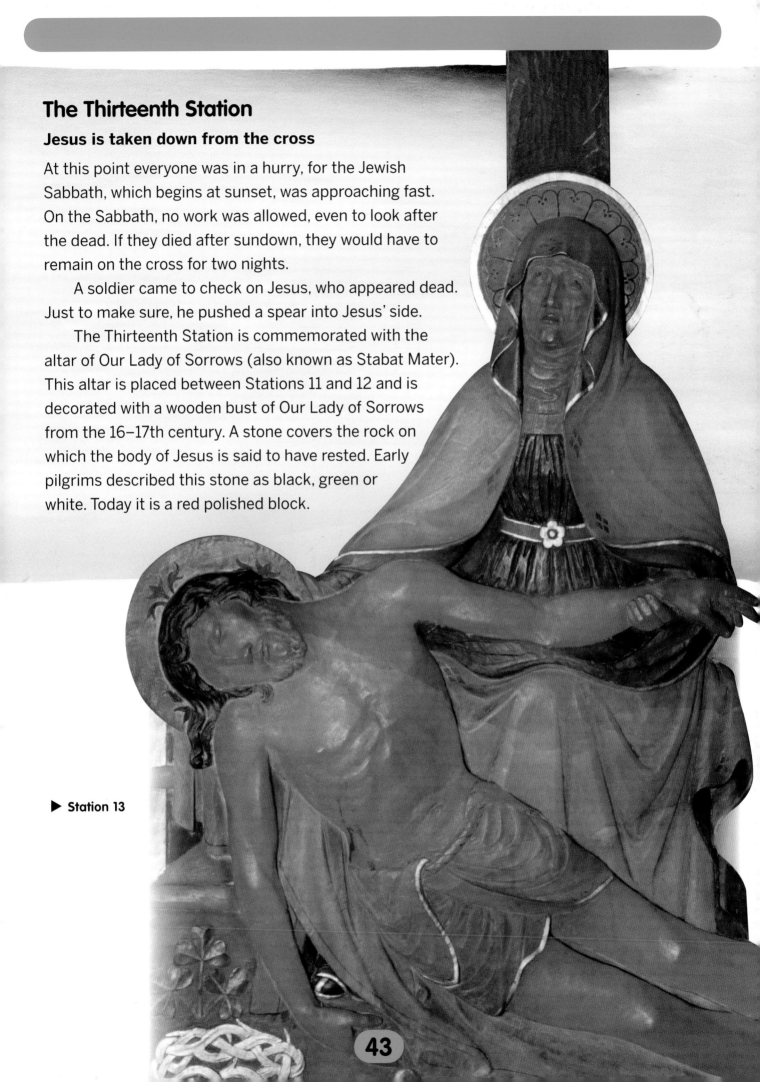

The Thirteenth Station

Jesus is taken down from the cross

At this point everyone was in a hurry, for the Jewish Sabbath, which begins at sunset, was approaching fast. On the Sabbath, no work was allowed, even to look after the dead. If they died after sundown, they would have to remain on the cross for two nights.

A soldier came to check on Jesus, who appeared dead. Just to make sure, he pushed a spear into Jesus' side.

The Thirteenth Station is commemorated with the altar of Our Lady of Sorrows (also known as Stabat Mater). This altar is placed between Stations 11 and 12 and is decorated with a wooden bust of Our Lady of Sorrows from the 16–17th century. A stone covers the rock on which the body of Jesus is said to have rested. Early pilgrims described this stone as black, green or white. Today it is a red polished block.

▶ Station 13

▼ Station 14

▲ Jesus is wrapped in burial clothes.

The Fourteenth Station

Jesus is laid in the tomb

After He was dead, the soldiers would have lowered the body to the ground and gone home. Their job was done. The Romans allowed locals to look after their own dead, even people who had been crucified were usually allowed burial according to local customs.

Mary Magdalene, Jesus' mother, Mary, and several other followers of Jesus were wondering what to do with His body; they had no tomb prepared. At this point, Joseph of Arimethea appeared, offering his tomb. He purchased fine linen and, helped by Nicodemus, he took the body and wrapped it in the fine linen, sprinkling it with myrrh and other spices that Nicodemus had brought. This would keep the body from decomposing too much until it could be properly prepared after the Sabbath.

The Resurrection

Jesus is now dead. But it is, of course, not the last time He will be seen on Earth, for this is the time of the Resurrection.

The day after the Sabbath, Mary Magdalene and Mary the mother of James, and another woman called Salome went to prepare Jesus' body for burial according to the Jewish tradition of the time.

As they approached the tomb, they began to wonder how they would roll away the large stone in front of the entrance, because it was very heavy. But then they saw the stone was already rolled back.

Entering the tomb, they saw a young man sitting on the right side, dressed in a white robe, and they were amazed. He said He knew that they were looking for Jesus, but that He was no longer there because He had risen. Instead they should tell His Disciples that He would meet them again in Galilee.

Of course, the women were terrified and fled out of the tomb. This event – that Jesus had been raised from the dead – is the foundation of the Christian Church.

The story of the Resurrection demonstrated that those who follow Jesus can indeed live forever with God. Jewish belief taught that on the Day of Judgement the dead would be resurrected. But the Day of Judgement would come at the end of time. The Resurrection of Jesus changed everything. It showed that there was

▲ The Resurrection is a common theme for religious works of art.

no need to wait for the Day of Judgement. All one had to do was commit completely to Jesus and follow His path and you could be resurrected in God immediately.

In the days and weeks that followed, Jesus came back to His closest followers. The first time was when the women went off to tell the Disciples, as they had been asked. It was on the road to Galilee and Jesus met them and greeted them. They bent down and worshipped Him and He told them not to be afraid.

Peter and some of the other Disciples went back to their jobs as fishermen. They had worked through the night but had not caught any fish at all. They were preparing to come back in with empty nets, when in the half-light of dawn they caught sight of someone standing on the shore. It was Jesus, but the Disciples did not recognise Him.

Jesus called out to them, "Friends, haven't you any fish?" "No," they answered. He said, "Throw your net on the right side of the boat and you will find some." When they did, they were unable to haul the net in because of the large number of fish. Then Simon Peter said, "It is the Lord!"

Simon Peter was so excited that he jumped in the water and swam to shore, while the others followed in the boat, hauling their huge catch of fish. When they landed, they saw a fire of burning coals there, and some bread. Jesus said to them, "Bring some of the fish you have just caught. Come and have breakfast." Jesus took the bread and gave it to them, and did the same with the fish.

The end of the story – and the beginning?

After this, the Disciples went to a mountain cave, where Jesus met with them and told them to teach His words to everyone they could, and to baptise them in the name of the Father, the Son and the Holy Spirit. However, John ends his Gospel in a very interesting way, by saying that there are many other things Jesus did and said, but that it is far too much to write down. It's almost like he is saying, "Stay tuned to this channel and I will tell you even more later on." And that, of course, is what Christians believe today.

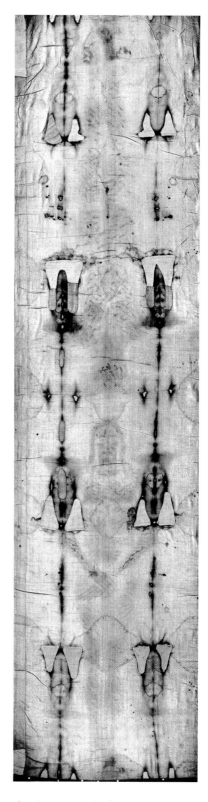

▲ The Shroud of Turin is a linen cloth bearing the image of a man who appears to have been crucified. It is kept in the royal chapel of the Cathedral of Saint John the Baptist in Turin, Italy. It is believed by many to be the cloth placed on Jesus at the time of His burial.

Glossary

BLASPHEMY The disrespectful use of the name of God.

COMMANDMENT An instruction from God. Christians recognise the Ten Commandments of the Old Testament plus further commandments given by Jesus during His ministry.

COMMUNION Something that is shared in common with others.

CRUCIFIXION The killing of a person by tying or nailing them to a cross.

DISCIPLES The students of Jesus. There were many student disciples, but Jesus selected 12 to be the Disciples (capital D).

GOSPEL The 'Good News'. The first four books of the New Testament: the Gospel of Matthew, Gospel of Mark, Gospel of Luke and Gospel of John.

HOLY WEEK The last week beginning the Sunday before Easter (Palm Sunday), up to Maundy Thursday (Holy Thursday) and Good Friday and the Saturday before Easter Day.

MESSIAH Jewish word for the saviour of Israel. The Greek word is Christ.

PASSOVER One of the most important Jewish holy days and festivals commemorating God sparing the Jews when He killed the first born of Egypt.

PHARISEES The 'pious ones', religious teachers of the Jewish community at the time of Jesus.

THE TEMPLE The main temple of the Jewish nation in Jerusalem. It had been founded by Kind David and built by King Solomon and rebuilt by King Herod.

Index

Agony of Jesus 23
Annas 16, 17

Barabbas 5, 19
blasphemy 5, 16, 17, 39, 48

Caiaphas 16, 17
Calvary 5, 25, 34, 36
commandments 9, 12, 48
communion 11, 48
crucifixion 4, 5, 29, 39, 48

Disciple 4, 6, 9, 11, 12, 13, 14, 47, 48

Garden of Gethsemane 4, 13, 14, 15, 23
Golgotha 5, 25, 34, 36
Good Friday 4, 5
Gospel 4, 9, 11, 48

Holy Sepulchre 22, 34
Holy Spirit 13
Holy Week 4, 48

Judas 4, 5, 11, 12, 14, 18

King of the Jews 19, 25, 39

Last Supper 4, 11–13

Mary 28, 39, 43–45
Messiah 7, 39, 48
Mount of Olives 4, 9

Passion 4, 23
Passion narratives 23
Passover 4, 5, 6, 11, 24, 48
Peter 4, 5, 12, 13, 14, 17, 18, 47
Pilate 5, 17, 18, 19, 24–25, 39

Resurrection 9, 46–47

Scriptural Way of the Cross 21, 22
Simon of Cyrene 29
Stations of the Cross 21–45

Temple 4, 6, 8, 34, 48

Veronica 30, 31
Via Dolorosa 20, 21, 22, 23